Regret, Sorrow, and Woe

Gemma Tansy

Presentation by *BookLeaf Publishing*

Web: www.bookleafpub.com

E-mail: info@bookleafpub.com

ISBN: 9789358313468

First edition 2023

DEDICATION

This book is dedicated to my nanna. Without you, this book would not be possible. You will never be forgotten and now you're memorialised between these pages. I hope I've made you proud.

ACKNOWLEDGEMENT

I want to make a moment to acknowledge my mum and how she's always pushed me to achieve my dreams. She's never given up on me and has always been my number one supporter, my best friend, my Cagney to my Lacey. I couldn't have done this without you.

I also want to thank my husband, my dad and Berty the pug for believing in me. Love you all.

The final goodbye

When I agreed to do this, I thought it would be
easy.

The last phone call,
Our last conversation,
Our last laugh,
Etched in my brain.

Cross words once exchanged
Melt away
Like ice in the warming winter sun
Giving this shadow of grief
Some warmth.

The three musketeers broken apart.
A promise kept by all parties.

I know you will be there
for us all
giving us that strength
and guidance
you once gave us in life.

Now death silences your once wise words
We have no choice

But to mimic our old tête-à-têtes
And to ponder
On fond memories.

Sleep well,
Nanna.
I love you.

One for sorrow…

One for sorrow.

Two for joy;
The slight relief knowing you were no longer
suffering and were back surrounded by those
that once loved you just as much as I.

Three for a girl;
Who were stood by your bedside as you took
your final breath, silently weeping.

Four for a boy;
The grieving husband you left behind.

Five for silver;
The covering of mirrors to let you go onwards
on your journey from this world to the next.

Six for gold;
Each swirl, curve and loop of your name
carefully engraved on the coffin plate, engraving
the fact that you had gone.

Seven for a secret, never to be told.

Just as you left it.

Your slippers are sat by your bedside, just as you left them.

Your coat still hanging up behind the front door, just as you left it.

The bottle of lemon juice you became obsessed with, sits collecting dust, unopened.

Your keys crumpled on the side, just as you left them.

Your rocking chair sits cold and stiff, covered in your crochet cushions, just as you left it.

The boxes of tablets and bottles of medicine now clear from sight, just as you would have wanted.

Your photos in a mix match of different size frames cover the walls and jumble the sides, just as you left them.

Your mug that you once sipped tea from remains perched on the shelf in the kitchen, just as you left it.

The pain of knowing I'll never get to hear your voice again or being able to tell you I love you one last time consumes me, just as much as the day you took your last breath as you left me.

Shockwaves

Gathering around your bedside and awaiting for you to take your inevitable last breath.

Obliging to your every last wish, no matter how difficult it was for us all.

Obediently organising your final send off, making sure it was something you would be proud of.

Decisively picking out your final outfit and small memorabilia's of your life to accompany you in your final journey.

Being able to see you one last time in your final resting place.

You looked so small laying there, with a slightly angry look upon your face - we knew you hated us being there, seeing you like that.

Even though we only got a moment alone, I got to say my final goodbye.

You.

On the day you left us;

The winds whipped - but
You lay still.

Sorrow swelled the room - but
You were ready to go.

Magpies flocked and cawed - but
You remained silent.

We were scared of the unknown - but
You were at peace.

The room was filled with chaos - but
You had an air of harmony about you.

But you, and only you, could have left this
hollow ache in our lives. One we will never be
able to fill, until we are reunited again.

As you were

I'd like to think you're in a garden,
surrounded by the most beautiful of flowers,
Where winter doesn't exist and the ground
doesn't harden,
You could frolic in the sun, for hours and hours.

I can see you standing there in your blue and red
Spider-Man dress,
Floating around the kitchen putting together a
roast,
Or tending to your pot of cress
That you enjoyed the most.

Your pride and joy would always be your
rocking chair,
With wool in one hand and in the other your
hooks,
Or having mum stand behind you putting a perm
in your hair,
We'd sit for hours talking and looking through
your stack of photo books.

You felt free when you played with paint,
A talented artist who never got to achieve her
dream,

When placed in front of a canvas showed no no
restraint,
The passion clearly flowed through her
bloodstream.

There was so much that you missed out on in
life,
but your personality is forever engraved here,
You may be known by others as Mrs Fyffe,
But now you're free to wonder and be sincere.

Anger

Anguish, despair and heartbreak fuel me,
Numbness towards the reality of it all.
Grieving for a woman whom I spent so many
years fighting,
Eventually realising that we were just too
similar.
Reliving the guilt of every cross word spoken at
every waking moment.

Bargaining

Being there, by your side right until the end, just
felt right.
After all, you'd been there looking after me
when I was younger.
Right in that last hour, all I could do was plead
to anyone listening,
God or otherwise.
All I wanted was a few more hours with you.
I was making promises that I couldn't keep
Negotiating with a being not present.
I'm the midst of it all, I forgot how selfish I was
being,
Not considering you in this selfish thought,and
failing to recognise that you were ready to
depart from this world.
Gone in your physical form, but always in our
hearts.

Denial

Denying all knowledge of what was happening
inside your body, slowly rotting and filling with
poison,
Even though the horrific truth had been staring
us in the face for a while.
Not willing to accept defeat, we made a pact as
the three musketeers to beat this.
In all honesty, I don't think any of us really
thought you'd succumb to this.
All too soon, our world began to crash and it
became apparent.
Losing you was the start of it all.

Depression

Deep in my mind, replaying every argument and
every bitter, spiteful word ever said.
Eternal purgatory, knowing I'd never get to
confirm that you'd forgiven me.
Pleading with your lifeless corpse to know that I
loved you deeply and that I was sorry.
Replaying our final conversation in my head,
there was so much more I wish I had said.
Eagerly wishing you could still hear me.
Sadness pulsated throughout my body.
Sorrow washed over me like a vigorous wave
plunging over a decaying piece of lifeless
driftwood.
In reality, I wasn't living, I was just existing.
Obeying my body's instruction to breathe, eat
and sleep.
Navigating this new "normal" without you,
never feeling complete again.

Acceptance

April flew by, and it wasn't until early May that we got to see you again.
Clean bedding was one of the first things we did after you passed, we know how much you would have hated a messy bed.
Choosing what outfit would be your last - knowing you'd go spare if we forgot your knickers.
Even putting in one of your crocheted pillows, so you'd be comfortable.
Preparing your speech, making sure that I was going to do you proud.
Talking to myself in every mirror possible, practicing my speech to make sure I didn't let you down.
Accepting at that final viewing that you were no longer here with us - just your shell remained.
Nothing could convince me otherwise that you were in that coffin, the sparkle that made you my nanna had been extinguished and set free.
Calmly leaving the viewing room, feeling lighter and happier knowing you weren't suffering anymore.
Expecting to forget that stench of lilies and decay, something which makes my nose shudder

at the mere thought of - purely the only sense
that ties me back to that room, grounding me
once more.

Yesterday, today, tomorrow.

Yesterday we were sat on your bed, and you were saying goodbye without neither of us wanting to acknowledge it.

Today we said goodbye in a physical sense, your flesh committed to the fire, surrounded by those that loved you the most.

Tomorrow your ashes will be scattered and set free to roam wherever you please - you are no longer conformed to a life of pain and misery.

From cradle, to the grave

First you were a daughter,
Then a devoted wife.

You then became a mother,
Only to give your life.

The title of Nanna was duly earnt,
That contained both harmony and strife.

Now you live on the cusp of this world and the next,
Sleep tight Mrs Fyffe.

Thanatophobia

Dying is something I've always been scared of.

It's the finality of it all.

One day, you wake up, not knowing it will be your last.

Either you carry on your day as normal until your heart finally stops beating or you just don't wake up at all.

One day, the people you love will wake up, not knowing it will be their last memory of you.

It's the finality of it all.

Death is something I've always been scared of.

Penitence

Regret is left with the living,
Once someone has passed, you're left with the
penitence of your actions.

Who would I have been if I'd spent more time
with you, soaking up your wisdom?

What memories would we have made that could
comfort me in this time of grief?

Where could our relationship had taken us if
only I'd accepted your love.

Why didn't I do more? The overwhelming sense
of guilt consumes me night after night.

How can I move on, not knowing if you have
forgiven me?

Since you've been gone

Since you've been gone, you've missed so much.
These last 7 months have flown by, but also time
still feels frozen.

We finally moved into our first home.
Putting pieces of your past together.
Birthdays have come and gone.
The annual Christmas card.
Your favourite, BBQs.
Your birthday.
Summer.

You & I

You were there for me, holding my hand whilst
we crossed the road, making sure I was safe.
I was there for you, holding your hand whilst
you crossed over from this word to the next,
making sure you were safe.

You were there for me, especially when I was
poorly, making sure I drunk plenty and was as
comfortable as could be.
I was there for you, especially on those bad
days, making sure you were hydrated and were
comfortable and warm.

You were there for me, protecting me from the
harsh reality and keeping me shielded from the
horrors of life.
I was there for you, making sure you weren't to
know the full truth of what was going to happen,
even though you were more prepared than the
rest of us.

You were there for me when I most needed you,
I just hope I was there for you when you most
needed me.

The cycle

Grief is a funny thing.
You start to mourn before the person you love is
gone, just to start the process off again after their
passing.
You agree to do things you will later regret and
will haunt you in dreams to come.
You think about the silly things, like making
sure the funeral directors take clean underwear
and give them a pillow so your loved one is
comfortable.
You distract yourself by planning the funeral,
only to be overwhelmed by emotion on the day.
You try and be there for those you love dearly,
but knowing there's nothing you can do.
You spend time obsessing over the times you
bickered and argued, and forget all the good
times.
Only when you think you're done, the cycle
starts again.

www.ingramcontent.com/pod-product-compliance
Lightning Source LLC
LaVergne TN
LVHW050504210726
843509LV00015BA/2988